The Park Loop Road

A Guide to Acadia National Park's Scenic Byway

To my parents, Ruth and Leo Thayer,
who first introduced me to the beauty
and wonder of Acadia National Park.

The Park Loop Road

A Guide to Acadia National Park's Scenic Byway

Written and Photographed by Robert A. Thayer

Down East Books

ISBN 978-0-89272-443-7

Designed by Lindy Gifford

Printed in China

DownEastBooks
www.nbnbooks.com
Distributed by
National Book Network
800-462-6420

Library of Congress Cataloging-in-Publication Data

Thayer, Robert A., 1947–
    The Park Loop Road : a guide to Acadia National Park's scenic byway/
    written & photographed by Robert Alan Thayer.
        p.   cm.
    Includes bibliographical references (p.   ).
    ISBN 0-89272-443-9   (pbk.)
    1. Acadia National Park (Me.)—Guidebooks. 2. Natural history—
Maine—Acadia National Park—Guidebooks. 3. Acadia National Park
(Me.)—Pictorial works. 4. Natural history—Maine—Acadia National
Park—Pictorial works.
F27.M9T48 1999
917.41'450443—dc21   98-49425
                                                              CIP

Contents

Acknowledgments

I would like to thank the following people, whose efforts have greatly contributed to the quality and accuracy of this book.

Mike, Joan, and Megan Furnari; Deb Wade; and Wanda Moran, who are all friends and naturalists at Acadia National Park. Ed Winterberg at Wildwood Stables. Debbie Dyer at the Bar Harbor Historical Society. Charlie Campo from the *Bangor Daily News*. Martha Harmon and Joyce Peterson at the Jackson Laboratory. Jaylene Roths from the Mount Desert Island Historical Society.

My appreciation, too, to the talented artists of the Historic American Engineering Record, for the use of their beautiful and accurate drawings. They include: David Haney, harlen d.Groe, Ed Lupyak, Sarah F. Desbiens, J. Shannon Barras, Kate E. Curtis, Joseph Korzenewski, Neil Maher, Todd Croteau, and Richard Quin.

A special thanks to Chris Cornell, Alice Devine, and Karin Womer for their editorial expertise. And thank you to my wife, Linda, whose constant love and support have made this book possible.

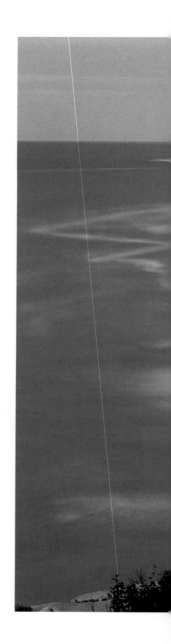

The ocean rolls in and explodes on the steep granite headlands in a powerful display of thunder and foam.

Fog filters through the evergreens and fills the air with the smell of balsam and spruce.

Rounded granite mountains rise above the forest, revealing views of a jagged coastline marching to the eastern horizon.

This is Mount Desert Island and Acadia National Park. From its dramatic geologic creation to the subtle, methodical forces that continue to mold its landscape, Acadia displays and preserves the beauty of Nature's story. People are drawn to this quiet landscape for play and relaxation, but here they also learn of the basic elements and complex laws of the natural environment.

This book is a guide to help you experience and appreciate the diversity of the natural and human history that are offered by Acadia's Loop Road, whether you travel in a car, on a bike, or on foot.

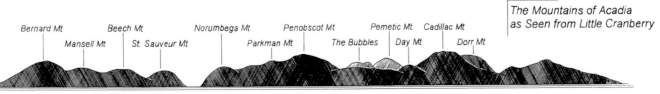

Bernard Mt   Beech Mt   Norumbega Mt   Penobscot Mt   Pemetic Mt   Cadillac Mt

Mansell Mt   St. Sauveur Mt   Parkman Mt   The Bubbles   Day Mt   Dorr Mt

The Mountains of Acadia as Seen from Little Cranberry

Bar Harbor was sparsely settled in the 1870s.

History of Mount Desert Island

Even before it was discovered by Europeans, Mount Desert Island was a special place for Native American people. Evidence of their activities here dates back nearly five thousand years. This early history is sketchy at best, but it is obvious that the island was used for its rich natural wealth. Hunting, fishing, clamming, and berry picking drew people to these shores. And, as today, the relatively mild climate—tempered by the Atlantic Ocean—allowed Native Americans who came to Mount Desert Island to escape the heat of summer or the bitter cold of winter.

On September 5, 1604, the French explorer Samuel de Champlain landed on Mount Desert. Noting that it was indeed an island, he made the following entry in his journal: "The mountain summits are all bare and rocky…. I name it *l 'Isles des Monts-déserts.*" In 1613, a French Jesuit settlement was established at the head of Somes Sound, but within weeks it was destroyed by the English.

For nearly one hundred and fifty years after its discovery, Mount Desert Island did not have a permanent settlement due to conflicts between the French and the English. It wasn't until 1760 that Abraham Somes and James Richardson established their families at what is now Somesville, which became the first permanent settlement on the island. Fishing, lumbering, shipbuilding, and farming were the occupations of the early residents. Hardy Yankee stock labored and prospered on this land so intimately connected to the sea.

In 1844, artist Thomas Cole visited Mount Desert Island. Although he was not the first to portray the area on canvas, Cole was, no doubt, the most influential. Because he was the leader of the Hudson River School, his paintings of Mount Desert attracted others to the coast of Maine. Scientists, religious leaders, and other artists came to the island to enjoy the natural beauty of

this coastal wonderland. Known as "rusticators," these early visitors would stay with the local people, eat their simple food, hike the mountains, canoe the lakes, and commune with the environment. It was said that they were living "the good life on a simple scale."

Because it was remote from the cities of the East yet within a few days' travel, many wealthy families found Mount Desert Island an ideal retreat, where the rules of high society were somewhat relaxed. By the 1880s, the atmosphere of the island had changed. Local inns and rooms-to-let were replaced with large hotels and elegant private "cottages." Elaborate dinner parties, afternoon teas, and formal dances replaced the day-long hikes, simple picnics, and rustic living of earlier days. Atwater Kent, a wealthy summer resident noted for hosting lavish social events, made the comment that this was "the good life on a grand scale."

Rusticators enjoy a Mount Desert summer.

George Dorr was the park's first superintendent.

Although the wealthy were responsible for the increased development of Mount Desert, it was through their efforts that preservation of the island began. In 1901, summer residents headed by Charles Eliot, president of Harvard, and George B. Dorr, a wealthy Bostonian, established the Hancock County Trustees of Public Reservations for the purpose of acquiring and preserving land for public use. In 1916, some five thousand acres were proclaimed Sieur de Monts National Monument by President Woodrow Wilson. George Dorr became its first superintendent. In 1919, it became Lafayette National Park, and in 1929 the name was changed to Acadia. Today the park encompasses more than forty thousand acres, preserving rocky shore, mixed woodlands, clear lakes, exposed mountaintops, and the rich human history of the area.

The Dane Cottage was one of Mount Desert's palatial summer homes.

The Loop Road

Until the early part of the twentieth century, automobiles were banned from Mount Desert Island. Southwest Harbor lifted the restriction in 1911, and Bar Harbor followed suit in 1913. By 1915, cars were allowed everywhere on the island, and it soon became necessary to provide roads to the newly formed national park. Between 1925 and 1941, the park service built the Loop Road with financial and technical support from John D. Rockefeller Jr.

Shaped by the expertise of noted landscape architect Frederick Law Olmstead Jr., it was designed to "...lead one through a series of visual experiences." Hence, the Loop Road does not draw attention to its own design and construction, but rather leads your eye to the beauty of nature and to the island itself.

This book will take you on a journey around Acadia's Loop Road. Your tour will begin as you leave the Visitor Center parking lot and proceed straight at the stop sign. This portion of the park road, completed in 1953, will connect to the loop section in about three miles. The speed limit is thirty-five miles per hour (except where posted otherwise), and at this speed you could, in theory, drive the twenty-mile loop in an hour.

However, if you take the time to see and experience just the stops discussed in this book, you may find that your visit could extend to a day, a week, or even a lifetime.

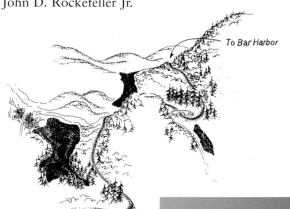

To Bar Harbor

To Seal Harbor

The Loop Road offers both elevated views . . .

. . . and sea-level vistas.

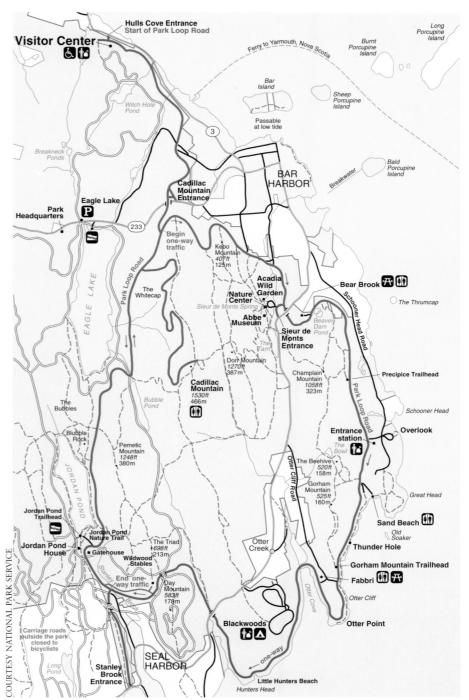

Hulls Cove Entrance
Start of Park Loop Road

Visitor Center

Long Porcupine Island

Burnt Porcupine Island

Ferry to Yarmouth, Nova Scotia

Bar Island

Sheep Porcupine Island

Witch Hole Pond

Passable at low tide

Breakneck Ponds

Bald Porcupine Island

③

BAR HARBOR

Breakwater

Cadillac Mountain Entrance

Park Headquarters

Eagle Lake
🅿

233

Begin one-way traffic

Kebo Mountain 407ft 125m

Acadia Wild Garden

Bear Brook 🏕 🚻

The Thrumcap

The Whitecap

Nature Center

Sieur de Monts Spring

Abbe Museum

EAGLE LAKE

Beaver Dam Pond

Sieur de Monts Entrance

Schooner Head Road

The Tarn

Dorr Mountain 1270ft 387m

Champlain Mountain 1058ft 323m

Precipice Trailhead

Cadillac Mountain 1530ft 466m 🚻

Bubble Pond

Schooner Head

The Bubbles

Entrance station 🚻

The Bowl

Overlook

Bubble Rock

Pemetic Mountain 1248ft 380m

The Beehive 520ft 158m

JORDAN POND

Gorham Mountain 525ft 160m

Great Head

Jordan Pond Trailhead

Sand Beach 🚻

Jordan Pond Nature Trail

The Triad 698ft 213m

Old Soaker

Otter Cliff Road

Thunder Hole

Jordan Pond House

Gatehouse

Wildwood Stables

Otter Creek

Gorham Mountain Trailhead

End one-way traffic

Day Mountain 583ft 178m

Fabbri 🚻 🏕

Otter Cliff

Blackwoods 🚻 🛆

Otter Cove

Otter Point

Stanley Brook

one-way

Carriage roads outside the park closed to bicyclists

Long Pond

SEAL HARBOR

Stanley Brook Entrance

Little Hunters Beach

Hunters Head

Frenchman Bay

The first stop on our tour is about a half-mile from the Visitor Center, just after the road divides. At the crest of the hill is a view-point that overlooks Frenchman Bay.

Frenchman Bay borders the east and north coasts of Mount Desert Island. The distant shore is the mainland, which includes the towns of Trenton, Lamoine, Hancock, Sorrento, Gouldsboro, and Winter Harbor. The mountains are the Gouldsboro hills, the largest of which is Schoodic Mountain.

As the bay's name reflects, there is a strong French heritage in this area. A Frenchman was credited with discovering the island, and until 1620, the area was known as New France. During the French and Indian War, the bay's many islands and jagged coastline provided ideal hiding places for French vessels seeking to avoid the British fleet. Today, reminders of the French linger in the place names throughout the island: Cadillac, St. Sauveur, Sieur de Monts, Huguenot Head, and Frenchman Bay are but a few.

From the mid-1700s to the mid-1800s, the bay was filled with ships of commerce. Bound for Europe and U.S. cities to the south, these vessels carried fish from rich local waters, lumber for building houses and boats, granite blocks for city buildings, and cobblestones for paving streets. When shipping traffic was at its peak, someone reportedly commented that it was possible to cross the harbor by jumping from one ship to the next. In the late 1800s and early 1900s, a new fleet of vessels arrived on the scene—the pleasure boats of wealthy families who came to enjoy the raw beauty and the relaxed lifestyle of the small coastal towns bordering the bay.

Today, the local finfish industry is in decline, lumber is no longer harvested, and no stone is quarried on the island. Nonetheless, Frenchman Bay continues to bustle with activity. Lobsterboats head out in the early hours of the morning to tend their traps. Pleasure craft ranging from kayaks to cabin cruisers travel its waters from Memorial Day to Labor Day. Tour boats filled with eager visitors circle the bay to view Mount Desert and to observe the wildlife that finds refuge on the smaller islands in the bay. Larger vessels venture farther from land in search of ocean birds and whales that feed in the rich offshore waters. And each summer, cruise ships the size of islands themselves enter the bay and proceed to the deep and friendly port in Bar Harbor.

Continuing onward 1.8 miles from the Frenchman Bay overlook, you will find a view-point on the left. From left to right, the panorama includes Frenchman Bay, then Champlain, Dorr, and Cadillac Mountains. Nearly everything in front of you and behind you was burned in 1947. The impact of the fire can be seen throughout the park, and it is etched in the memories and attitudes of the local people.

The bay's many islands and irregular coastline once provided hideouts for French warships.

The flames left nothing in their wake but chimneys.

Fighting the blaze was a losing battle.

The Great Fire

Nineteen forty-seven is often referred to as "The Year Maine Burned." The weather was very dry, with no rain from May to October. By fall, there had been many fires throughout the state, but none was as newsworthy as the blaze that started on Mount Desert Island. Listen to the words of Captain John Heath and Chief David Sleeper of the Bar Harbor Fire Department.

Friday, October 17, 1947, 4:05 P.M.: "A call to the Fire Department was received from Dolliver's Dump...about seven miles from the outskirts of town."

What was to become a massive firestorm began as a small, persistent fire near the dump in the northwest corner of the island.

Tuesday, October 21, dawn: "A brisk wind sprang up from the northwest and the chief...saw instantly the seriousness of the situation.... It was impossible to lay hose fast enough to reach the head of the fire."

Strong gusts pushed the flames across the island, engulfing everything in their path. On October 23, the wind shifted, and the fire raced toward the town of Bar Harbor.

Thursday, October 23 ("the most fateful day in Bar Harbor history"): "The velocity of the wind has been...reported at 40, 45, 50 or more miles an hour."

"It is remarkable that many people were not burned to death for the fire, stirred to a full inferno...descended upon the outskirts of the town."

"It looked as if two gigantic doors had opened and towering columns of roaring flames shot down upon [us]."

"The Belmont Hotel was in the cellar just twenty minutes from the time it caught afire."

"...The conflagration is indicated by the fire's sudden enormous expansion from approximately 1,900 acres at 4:00 P.M. to over 16,000 by midnight."

As the flames approached ever closer, local residents rushed down to the town dock and waited to be rescued by boat. Fortunately, at the last minute, the wind shifted again, sparing Bar Harbor itself. However, the raging fire destroyed no fewer than sixty-seven large estates on "Millionaires' Row," consumed one hundred seventy homes, and razed five large historic hotels.

Friday, October 24: *"[The day] dawned beautifully clear and quiet as though nature was seeking to make up for the terrible things she had done to us the night before."*

On October 27, the fire was declared under control, and three days later it was pronounced out. It had burned more than seventeen thousand acres of forest, ten thousand of them in Acadia. Property damage exceeded twenty-three million dollars, five people died in fire-related accidents, and the lives of the island's residents were changed forever.

At first glance it may appear that the great fire of 1947 put an end to Bar Harbor's romantic Cottage Era. That, however, is a misconception. The truth is that the institution of federal income taxes in 1913, the Great Depression of the 1930s and 1940s, and two world wars had already combined to redistribute the wealth of the nation. Long before the 1947 fire, many of Bar Harbor's elite had lost their money, and their estates had fallen into disrepair. The flames that swept the island served only as the dramatic, final blow.

Hardwoods have replaced the evergreens destroyed in the fire.

This colorful display of foliage is a product of the fire. Before 1947, Mount Desert was dominated by an evergreen forest of spruce and fir. Growing in its wake are the broad-leaved maple, aspen (poplar), oak, and beech trees we see today. The color of this scene marks the fire's path and serves as a reminder of its awesome power. From today's vantage point, we are reminded of Nature's ability to recover and persevere.

In the shade of these trees grow the young spruce and firs that will eventually reclaim their dominance of the island.

A left at the next intersection leads to Route 233 and into Bar Harbor. The second intersection marks the beginning of the loop section of the park road. A left here will take you to Ocean Drive. *Traffic is one-way only.* The right lane is used for parking and the left lane for travel, unless otherwise posted. Many of the view-points also serve as trailheads for those wishing to explore the park in a more intimate and personal way.

The first view-point reveals Bar Harbor and is the beginning of the North Ridge Trail up Cadillac Mountain.

Cadillac Mountain looks down on the town of Bar Harbor.

Bar Harbor

The town of Bar Harbor grew around this area of deep, protected water. Historically, the population fluctuated with the seasons, as Native Americans took advantage of the moderate climate along the coast. The present is no exception. Winter finds a small, stable population of year-round residents. As summer approaches, the streets swell with hundreds of seasonal shop owners, thousands of summer residents, and millions of visitors. Each spring, Bar Harbor experiences a complete metamorphosis—from quiet coastal village to bustling resort Mecca—and each fall, the process is reversed.

The harbor itself is dominated by five small islands called the Porcupines, named for their humped shape and the quill-like trees that adorn their backs. From left to right as viewed in the accompanying photograph, they are: Bar Island, Sheep Island, Burnt Island, Long Island, and Bald Island. Bald, Sheep, and most of Bar are now part of Acadia National Park, which protects their unique habitats as well as the bald eagles and osprey that nest on them.

Low tide reveals the source of Bar Harbor's name. For several hours each day, the tide exposes a broad sandbar between Bar Harbor and Bar Island, making the latter accessible by foot or automobile. Sections of the island are still privately owned by residents who must plan their lives around the ebb and flow of the tide.

Strangely enough, the Porcupine Islands—including Bar—are part of the town of Gouldsboro, across the bay.

For the next mile, the Loop Road winds downward into a forested valley. The view then opens onto Great Meadow and to Dorr and Cadillac Mountains on the right. Follow the signs to Sieur de Monts Spring. Here you will find the park's Nature Center, the Abbe Museum, the Wild Gardens of Acadia, and the spring itself.

Bar Island (foreground) is accessible from Bar Harbor at low tide.

Great Meadow is a good place for bird-watching.

The Spring House survived the fire of 1947.

Sieur de Monts Spring

Purchased in 1909 by George Dorr in a dramatic, last-minute deal, Sieur de Monts Spring and the land surrounding it became an important acquisition for the growing preservation movement on Mount Desert. It was named after the proprietor of the first French colony in North America, Pierre du Guast, Sieur de Monts.

Dorr commissioned the construction of the octagonal cover house over the spring and had a nearby stone inscribed with the words, "The Sweet Waters of Acadia." As much as any place in the park, Sieur de Monts Spring serves as a memorial to George Dorr, whose love of the island was the driving force behind the creation of Acadia National Park.

At the center of this area is the Nature Center, a wooden building housing a number of exhibits relating to the plants and animals found in Acadia. Books and information about the park may also be obtained here.

Abbe Museum was founded by Robert Abbe, a New York surgeon whose interest in local Indian history led to the first archaeological excavations along the coast of Maine. Each summer, in addition to the exhibits, the museum sponsors educational demonstrations, research, and conservation programs. There is a modest entrance fee to the museum, which is not operated by Acadia National Park and must support itself.

Because of its wet, wooded location, Sieur de Monts Spring is an ideal spot for bird-watching, especially during spring and fall migrations.

Wild Gardens of Acadia

Across from the Nature Center is the entrance to these extraordinary gardens.

In 1961, the Bar Harbor Garden Club took on the task of creating a showcase for the native plants of Acadia. On this three-quarter-acre plot, the garden is divided into twelve distinct habitats, from woodland to meadow, sand dune to mountaintop. Throughout the spring, summer, and fall, a parade of flowers and trees bloom, mature, and go to seed here. The Wild Gardens are a living guide to the botanical variety of Acadia: Use them to predict what might be in bloom in the park or as a reference to the identity of plants you've seen along the trails you walk.

Upon leaving the Wild Gardens and Sieur de Monts Spring, follow the signs back to the Loop Road, and take a right (remember, this is a one-way road). Within a short distance, you will see the Bear Brook Picnic area on your left, and just beyond that—on the right—is a small, unmarked body of water called Beaver Dam Pond.

The large building across the street from the pond is the Jackson Laboratory, which is world renowned for its genetically engineered mice and for its medical research. The lab is the largest employer on the island.

Sheep Laurel

Yellow Loosestrife

Cardinal flower

Blue Flag

Balsam-fir cones

Purple-fringed Orchid

Beaver Dam Pond

Nestled at the foot of Champlain Mountain, this small round pond is home to beavers, river otters, ducks, and a myriad of plants and smaller animals. Signs of beaver activity are everywhere. Although these animals are most active at night, dams, lodges and freshly chewed trees are clear indicators of their presence. Here they have created and maintain a habitat that not only serves their needs, but also provides food and homes for an entire community of organisms.

In building dams to maintain the pond's water level, the beaver may threaten manmade structures. This can test the creative abilities of the park's resource managers to preserve buildings and roads while allowing the beaver to express its natural instincts. Because the sound of moving water stimulates beavers to build dams, a properly placed overflow pipe can quietly lower the level of the pond without arousing their urge to rebuild.

Early morning and evening are the best times to observe beavers and other wildlife at the pond. Ducks and many species of songbirds commonly feed and nest in this area. Deer often come to drink from the pond and to eat the young plants that grow along its wet borders. The secretive river otter may play in the reeds at the edge of the pond. A bald eagle may perch atop an open tree looking for fish in the shallow water.

Warning: Although most wildlife species found in the park are non-threatening, these are still "wild" animals and should not be approached or fed. This warning includes chipmunks, squirrels, raccoons, foxes, and gulls. These animals may be cute and may even beg, but they will become pests when encouraged by handouts. If a wild animal approaches you on its own, it may be sick or diseased, and should be avoided. Observe wildlife from a distance in their natural habitat.

As you resume your tour of the Loop Road, it will crest a hill after Beaver Dam Pond. Here, the view opens to a panorama of the entrance to Frenchman Bay. As you descend the hill, notice the large brick building below and on your left.

The beavers have created ideal wildlife habitat.

Chisel teeth make short work of large trees.

The beautiful mansion has a tragic and romantic history.

Highseas

Highseas is the only "cottage" on this section of the island to survive destruction by the fire of 1947. It was built in 1912 by Princeton professor Rudolph Brunnow for his bride-to-be. Unfortunately, she was traveling to this country on the *Titanic* and was lost at sea. Professor Brunnow continued to summer in the cottage, and it was he who laid out the Precipice Trail up Champlain Mountain. Ironically Professor Brunnow fell while climbing and later died of complications from the accident.

In 1924, a New Yorker named Eva Van Cortland Hawkes bought the house and named it Highseas after it weathered a particularly rough storm. Mrs. Hawkes's dedicated gardener saved the structure from the 1947 fire by continuously hosing it down in the face of the advancing flames. Highseas was given to the Jackson Laboratory in 1951. Today, it serves as a dormitory for students who work at the research facility.

Just down the hill from the Highseas overlook, on the right, you'll find the parking area for the Precipice Trail.

Precipice Trail

The Precipice Trail on the east face of Champlain Mountain may be the most challenging and most popular trail in the park. It is less than a mile long, but what it lacks in length, it more than makes up for in vertical challenge. This is not just a hike but a climb, requiring both feet and hands. Iron rungs and ladders provide assistance in some of the steeper sections, but even with their help, the Precipice Trail is not for the unprepared nor for those who fear heights.

The sheer face of Champlain Mountain was created as glaciers passed over its summit and pulled granite blocks from its southeastern slope. These boulders were either deposited at the base of the mountain, creating a talus slope, or carried into the sea. This same process has shaped all of the peaks on the island; Champlain Mountain and the Precipice Trail are merely the most obvious examples.

Hiking access to the trail may be restricted during certain periods. In 1984–86 falcon chicks were reintroduced to Mount Desert Island at Jordan Cliffs, on the side of Penobscot Mountain. Since 1991, peregrines have regularly established nesting sites on Champlain's face, and the trail is closed each year (anywhere from March through mid-August) until the chicks leave the nest. The trailhead is still a popular stop for those wishing to watch the young chicks learn to perform their aerial aerobatics.

The next left, just before the fee station, will take you to an overlook that offers a fine view of Frenchman Bay.

The Precipice Trail cuts across the sheer face of Champlain Mountain.

Egg Rock

The small rocky island at the mouth of Frenchman Bay is called Egg Rock. Named because of the large number of nesting birds there, the island also sports a lighthouse that is the most visible of all those along the Loop Road. (Farther on, Baker Island Light can also be seen with sharp eyes or binoculars.) If the weather is foggy, you may not see the light or the lighthouse, but you will most definitely hear the fog horn that persistently warns of the island's presence.

Egg Rock Light was built in 1875 to coincide with Bar Harbor's emergence as a popular resort area. It was automated in 1977 and is now periodically maintained by the Coast Guard. Though no longer inhabited by humans, the island is home to colonies of laughing gulls; Common, Arctic, and Roseate terns; and harbor seals that lounge on its rocky edges.

Across the bay is Schoodic Peninsula, which is also part of Acadia National Park. Although its distance from this view-point is only about five miles as the crow flies, by road it is forty-five miles away—an hour's drive from Bar Harbor. If you have the time, the trip is worth the effort. Directions and further information can be obtained at the Acadia Visitor Center.

The large private house seen from this view-point is on Schooner Head. It was built in the 1980s and is not one of the old historic cottages. This structure is, however, a reminder that Acadia, unlike most other national parks, was formed from land donated by generous citizens and that today the park shares the island with a number of towns and parcels of private property.

A short distance beyond the fee station is the parking area for Sand Beach. In the large lower lot are restrooms and changing houses. The second, upper parking lot is intended for those who want to walk the Ocean Trail.

Egg Rock Light lies between Bar Harbor and Winter Harbor.

The island plays host to both harbor seals and pelagic birds.

Sand Beach is one of the most popular spots in Acadia National Park.

Sand Beach and the Ocean Trail

On warm, sunny days this is the most popular spot in the park. A sandy beach is a rare find on an otherwise rocky coastline and is an irresistible magnet for sun lovers and those escaping the heat inland. However, you will rarely see large numbers of people actually in the water, as its temperature seldom reaches above 60°F.

Take a close look at the "sand" here, and you will discover its source. More than half the beach consists of crumbled clam shells, mussel shells, and green sea-urchin spines. This gives the sand a unique texture and appearance, and you'll find that it sticks to everything. Sand Beach lies at the end of Newport Cove, and "Old Soaker," the small rock island at the mouth of the cove, helps to direct the current that deposits sand and shells on the shore.

On the far side of the beach is a massive granite peninsula called Great Head, one of the highest headlands on the Atlantic Coast. A trail from the beach climbs the 145-foot wall, and a path that crosses the peninsula provides views along the shore and out into Frenchman Bay. This is also an excellent location to explore the exciting bedrock geology of Mount Desert Island.

Behind the beach is a brackish lagoon created by a berm of sand. This barrier has a tentative life, as winter storms often pull the sand back out to sea. When the berm breaks, the warm fresh water of the lagoon rushes into the ocean, and the salt water moves inland, thus rejuvenating the marsh. This dune environment is fragile. Please observe it from a distance, and leave the grasses undisturbed so that they may do their job of anchoring the sand.

From the far side of the beach, you can see the rounded Beehive, a small but impressive mountain shaped by the passing glaciers. Its southeast-facing slope is rugged and precipitous. A short, steep climb leads to the summit, where the views along the coast are well worth the effort. An alternate, less strenuous trail will take you to a small pond, called the Bowl, and up the gentler back side of the Beehive.

The Ocean Trail begins at the far end of the upper parking lot at Sand Beach. This 1.8-mile walk follows the shore to Otter Point and provides an intimate way to experience the rocky coast. A flat and easy trail, it traverses one of the most spectacular and accessible sections of the Maine coast. Along the way, you will encounter Thunder Hole, Monument Cove, and Otter Cliffs.

Photo tip: This east-facing side of the island is best photographed in the morning, when the early sun lights the pink granite.

The Beehive was sculpted by glaciers.

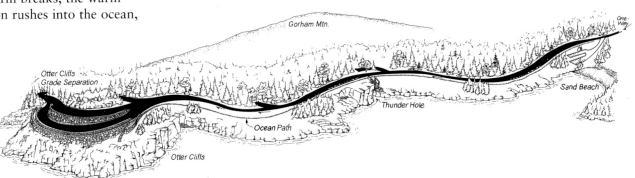

Thunder Hole

Plan to arrive at Thunder Hole midway between low and high tide, when it is most active. This geological phenomenon is especially impressive after a storm has passed out to sea, and during these periods of large waves, its thunder can be heard for several miles. When the tide and the surf are right, Thunder Hole earns its name and its reputation, rivaling Yellowstone's Old Faithful in its drama but not in its predictability. Most of the time, however, the rise and fall of gentle waves creates only a low rumble.

What makes the sounds heard here? Thunder Hole is essentially a crack, or chasm, in the granite within the intertidal zone. At the end of this chasm is a small cave. As waves surge into the chasm, their speed increases; air is trapped and compressed in the cave; and with no place to go, the water and air are forced out and up with a thunderous roar.

About half a mile from Thunder Hole is a small, unmarked cove indicated by a low stone wall overlooking a boulder beach. Just beyond is the parking area for Gorham Mountain.

At its best, the roar of Thunder Hole is truly impressive.

. . . and continues to shape its stones.

Monument Cove

When the sea works its way into the land, small crescent-shaped coves add another dimension to the shoreline. Such indentations are created where the granite bedrock is in a cracked and weakened condition, making it susceptible to the relentless advances of the sea.

As you view Monument Cove with its steep granite cliffs, look carefully against the left wall for a twenty-foot-high marine stack standing alone and erect. This is the "monument," for which this place was named. The pillar was created as the ocean selectively eroded the weaker rock from its base—proof that the hardness of granite is no match for the persistence of the sea. Much of the rock eroded from the shore now forms a boulder beach on the floor of the cove.

Beyond Monument Cove, the Loop Road offers spectacular views of Otter Cliffs. Rising one hundred ten feet directly from the ocean, these bluffs represent one of Acadia's quintessential scenes.

Wave action created the pillar at Monument Cove . . .

Otter Cliffs

When the surf is high, the waves crash dramatically on this wall of granite, often splashing twenty to thirty feet above the cliffs themselves. On calmer days, you are likely to see climbers pitting their skills against the rock face. If you have the time, you might want to find a spot near the shore and simply enjoy the sights, sounds, and smells of the ocean.

Notice the change in vegetation from this point on. This is where the 1947 fire reached its terminus. The trees at the end of Otter Point are large, mature red spruce that stand in sharp contrast to the sparse, low, deciduous vegetation found on the rest of Ocean Drive. If you are hiking the trail on a warm day, you will feel the difference as you enter the cool, dark evergreen forest.

Facing due east from the top of Otter Cliffs, you will see a small rocky shoal marked by a bell buoy. At mid-tide, the waves play with this ledge, which is often mistaken for a whale. (In the log of Champlain's first voyage to this area, he mentions running aground on a rock ledge, and it was most likely this one.) The view back toward Sand Beach displays the entire shoreline along Ocean Drive.

Are there otters at Otter Point and Otter Cliffs?

There are certainly river otters on Mount Desert, and they may occasionally be found in the ocean. But, there are no sea otters on the East Coast. The reference to otters in these place names is most likely linked to the now-extinct sea mink. This fur-bearing mammal was a larger and more robust relative of the common mink and was locally called an otter. Hunted for its fur, the sea mink disappeared in the 1860s.

At Otter Point, a little walking and climbing will provide you with access to the shore and its intertidal zone, which is quite dramatic at low tide. Park your car in the lot on the right, and walk across the street to the Ocean Trail and Otter Point. Along the trail look for openings to the shore.

Surf crashes on the shore along Ocean Drive.

Tall red spruce trees top dramatic Otter Cliffs.

Common Periwinkles

Northern Rock Barnacles

The intertidal gradient consists of five distinct zones.

Bladder Wrack

Otter Point

As you walk from the forest toward the sea, you will cross a barren stretch of pink granite that forms the shoreline here. Below this is the intertidal zone, a twelve-foot area between the tides where life changes from terrestrial to aquatic.

At high tide, the zone is under several feet of cold, foamy salt water; six hours later, it is exposed to the hot, drying sun. Even with these extremes, life not only exists but flourishes here. In his book *The Rocky Shore,* John Kingsbury describes the intertidal zone as having the "beneficence of adversity." Once adapted to the contrast between high and low water, organisms in this zone can take advantage of the best that each world has to offer.

The intertidal gradient actually consists of five identifiable zones. Starting with the one lying farthest inland and moving seaward, they are:

1. The spray zone. At high tide, this nearly terrestrial area is subjected to a fine, salty spray, and only a few algae and lichens can survive such Spartan conditions. Small Rough Periwinkles eke out an existence by feeding on these simple plants and finding protection in the cracked granite bedrock. Enter this black spray zone carefully because when they're wet, the rocks are as slippery as if they were covered with oil.

2. The barnacle zone. Barnacles can only exist in places that high tide reaches every day. When covered with water, they stretch their feathery feet and feed on tiny plankton that they filter from the incoming sea. Though they may appear dead at low tide, barnacles are very much alive, each sustained by a single drop of water inside its limestone home. Mussels vie for space in this competitive zone, and dogwinkles scour the area, preying on both barnacles and mussels.

3. The rockweed zone. As a group, seaweeds are the trees of the intertidal zone. At high water, these giant algae sway with the ebb and flow of the surf. When the tide drops, they cover the rocks, creating a wet, gelatinous blanket under which a multitude of organisms survive until the next high tide.

4. Irish Moss zone. This area is exposed only at low tide. Irish Moss is not actually a moss but small bundles of reddish seaweed. Delicate sea lettuce adds a splash of green to this ruddy zone. Although not particularly appetizing in this form, most of these seaweeds are quite edible. The Irish Moss zone is a rich environment that provides food and shelter for a large number of marine organisms.

5. The kelp zone. Even at low tide, this zone is underwater. The long, leathery strands of kelp provide food and shelter for sea stars, sea urchins, and sea cucumbers, all of which are truly aquatic and must be submerged to survive.

As dramatic as the tidal range is on Mount Desert Island, farther north, in the Bay of Fundy, it is even more impressive. Here, the sea is squeezed into the narrow opening between Maine and Nova Scotia, and the tides rise and fall an amazing thirty feet.

After Otter Point, the Loop Road crosses Otter Cove on a causeway.

Seaweeds

Green Sea Urchin

Sea Star

Causeway and Otter Cove

It was into this cove that Champlain sailed on September 5, 1604, to repair his ship after hitting the rocky ledge off Otter Cliffs. It was also here that the French explorers may have met the Wabanaki Indians who inhabited this land, which they called Pemetic. No doubt such encounters were welcomed by Champlain's men, as they were seeking information about Norumbega, a mythical city of gold thought to be somewhere in the area.

The causeway that now crosses the cove was completed in 1939 by the Bureau of Public Roads. It connects the Ocean Drive section of the road to the Blackwoods stretch and truly makes this route a loop.

Here, low tide exposes a shallow mudflat where shorebirds and gulls hunt for mussels and snails, as well as small fish that have been stranded by the retreating tide.

Driving a short distance beyond the causeway, you will see three small view-points on the left, overlooking the open ocean. Facing the water there, you are looking due south, into the Gulf of Maine.

The arched-stone causeway was built in 1939.

OTTER CREEK COVE BRIDGE AND CAUSEWAY   1938

The Gulf of Maine is one of the most beautiful bodies of water on the Atlantic Coast.

Gulf of Maine

Down east Maine is the easternmost region on the U.S. mainland. The term "down east" has its roots in the days when sailing was the primary mode of transportation along the coast. If you were traveling from Boston to Mount Desert, you would be sailing downwind and to the east—or *down east*. If you headed due south from this point (approximately 68° West Longitude), the next major landfall would be just west of Caracas, Venezuela.

The islands in the distance are Baker and Little Cranberry; beyond them lies the open Atlantic

Ocean or, more precisely, the Gulf of Maine. Enclosed on three sides by the coasts of Maine, Nova Scotia, and Cape Cod, this body of water comprises a unique marine habitat.

Offshore banks and ledges limit the flow of the warm Gulf Stream into the Gulf of Maine. The icy Arctic water of the Labrador Current sweeps south around Nova Scotia and is the dominant influence on the gulf environment. The combination of cold water, relatively shallow depths, and slightly lowered salinity creates a

rich habitat for microorganisms like plankton. These tiny creatures form the base of the food chain that feeds the forage fish, which in turn attract larger prey species and fishermen to these bountiful waters.

After leaving this overlook, you will briefly reenter the woods, and in a short distance there will be a very small pull-over on the right. Across the street is a series of steep, wooden steps that lead down to a small boulder beach.

Little Hunters Beach

Little Hunters Beach is another of the Loop Road's unmarked treasures. Like Monument Cove, it was created by the force of the sea and the influence of the glaciers. The stones that comprise the beach are smooth and round, and are known as cobbles. Some of these come from the surrounding granite bedrock, while others were carried here by moving water and melting ice.

This beach is typical of those found along the Maine coast. Although its bedrock is very old, the shoreline was only recently exposed, after the retreat of the last continental glacier. For twelve thousand years, the sea has been pouring its energy into small inlets like this one, turning granite blocks to rounded cobbles. Listen carefully to the clicking sound as the waves tumble the stones into perfect oval shapes. Winter storms toss them high up on the beach, creating a berm or dune of pebbles and cobbles.

Early mariners used such stones as ballast for their ships. The cobbles later became a commodity, sold for profit and used to pave the streets of the growing cities in southern New England. Modern-day visitors may be the greatest threat to Maine's cobble beaches, because the stones leave one by one in the hands of thousands of uninformed collectors. Please remember: it is illegal to remove cobbles or anything else from the park! Leave Acadia as you found it, for future generations to enjoy.

After Little Hunters Beach, the Loop Road comes to a promontory called Hunters Head. The overlook on the left provides a view of the Great Harbor of Mount Desert.

These surf-sculpted boulders are known as cobbles.

Tide pools hold a microcosm of sea life.

Little Hunters is a classic New England cobble beach.

Across the busy passage known as the Eastern Way lie the Cranberry Isles.

Hunters Head

Locally referred to as the Great Harbor of Mount Desert, the body of water seen from this viewpoint encompasses the towns of Seal Harbor, Northeast Harbor, and Southwest Harbor, as well as the communities on Little and Great Cranberry Islands. On nearly every summer day, this bay teems with activity: lobstermen tending their traps; transport vessels of all shapes and sizes carrying supplies and people to the offshore islands; and schooners, sloops, ketches and yawls playing with the wind and competing with each other.

The islands that lie to the south are collectively called the Cranberry Isles: Baker, Little Cranberry, Great Cranberry, Sutton, and Bear. Look closely between Hunters Head and Little Cranberry Island; there you will see a small white day marker perched on a rock outcropping known as East Bunker's Ledge. Erected in 1804, the marker helps sailing vessels avoid this treacherous rock. Harbor seals and gray seals are drawn to this ledge because of its proximity to their feeding grounds and its isolation from human interference.

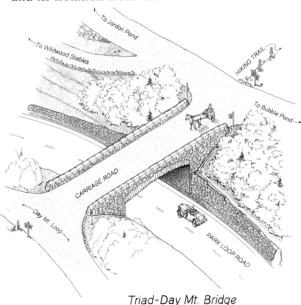

Triad-Day Mt. Bridge

Beyond Hunters Head, the Loop Road enters a mature evergreen forest, winding its way toward the center of the island. This area was not burned in 1947 and is a reminder of what all of Mount Desert was like before the great fire.

The road passes under two granite bridges, the second of which is the Triad–Day Mountain Bridge. It was built by the Park Service in 1941 to separate motor traffic from the system of carriage roads on the eastern half of the park. The right turn after this bridge is the entrance to Wildwood Stables, formerly the farm associated with the Dane Estate in Seal Harbor. In 1948, Helen Dane donated the eighty-seven-acre parcel to the park. It now serves as a concession where you can pay for a scenic ride in a horse-drawn carriage.

Acadia's carriage roads are part of the unique cultural heritage of Mount Desert Island. Their conception and construction were integral to the growth and development of the park itself.

In an effort to preserve the pristine nature of the surroundings, John D. Rockefeller Jr. supervised the design and construction of a fifty-seven-mile-long system of carriage roads throughout the eastern half of the island. From 1913 through 1940, he purchased the land, paid for the roads, and donated them to the growing national park. Today, those who travel these byways—whether by carriage, on foot, or on a bicycle—find themselves transported back in time and into the heart of Acadia, much of it shaped by Rockefeller's vision.

Born in 1874, he first visited Mount Desert Island with his family in 1908, when they rented a cottage in Bar Harbor. Two years later, Rockefeller acquired property in Seal Harbor—the Eyrie—which eventually grew into a massive one-hundred-room estate. It was also at this time that his life took a different direction: Rockefeller chose to dedicate himself to philanthropy. He

Wildwood Stables provides carriage rides.

would become one of Acadia's greatest benefactors. His involvement gave both substance and direction to the growing park. By the time he died, his gifts to Acadia included not only the carriage roads but also two gate lodges, sixteen stone bridges, 11,300 acres of land, Jordan Pond House and restaurant, technical and monetary support for construction of the Loop Road, and many millions of dollars in general donations.

But Rockefeller's contribution transcends the physical. His demonstration that the hand of man can be gentle and need not conflict with the works of Nature will no doubt be his most enduring legacy.

Just beyond the sign to the stables is an exit to Seal Harbor. To continue on the Loop Road, stay to the right. In a short distance, there will be a large stone house on your right.

Jordan Pond Gate Lodge

Commissioned in 1932 by John D. Rockefeller Jr., this gatehouse (and another in Northeast Harbor) serves as an entry point to the carriage-road system.

In order to find the appropriate design for these lodges, Rockefeller had his architect, Grosvenor Atterbury, visit western parks to study similar structures. Based on this trip, Atterbury established a set of principles as to how man-made structures should fit into a natural landscape: They should be unobtrusive and should not compete with their surroundings. And, if possible, they should be built of local materials and should reflect local traditions. Because Atterbury had no indigenous historical buildings as guides, he chose a design similar to a European hunting lodge. The natural landscaping around the gatehouses was conceived by noted landscape architect Beatrix Ferrand, who also summered on the island.

In the early 1930s one of Rockefeller's engineers, Paul Simpson, lived in the Jordan Pond gatehouse with his family. Today, it houses park personnel.

Across the street from the lodge is the Jordan Pond House and gift shop. Parking is limited here, but if you continue just down the road and turn left, you'll find a larger parking area. From this lot, a short wooded walk will bring you back to the restaurant. This same left ends at the boat ramp and provides access to Jordan Pond and the surrounding area.

The gatehouse was patterned after a European hunting lodge.

Jordan Pond

Bordered on three sides by mountains, Jordan Pond looks like a high alpine lake. This is merely an illusion, for in two miles its waters drop 270 feet to the ocean. Unlike most alpine lakes, Jordan Pond is a deep and productive body of water. It was, however, formed by glaciers—the same force that created alpine lakes. As the continental ice sheet was melting, a small glacier lingered in this valley, depositing a mound of rock and clay at its southern end. It is this mound (moraine) that blocked the flow of water out of the valley and created the deep pond. Its pristine waters attract canoeists, kayakers, and fishermen. However, swimming is not allowed, as Jordan Pond is a source of drinking water for the town of Seal Harbor.

At the northern end of the pond are two glacially rounded mountains called the Bubbles, perched between Penobscot and Pemetic Mountains. From Jordan's southern shore, the Bubbles appear to be symmetrical and equal in size, but in reality North Bubble is taller and farther away, with an elongated northern ridge. Mirrored in the clear waters of Jordan Pond, the Bubbles provide one of the most sublime views in the park.

Understandably, all the trails in this area seem to converge on Jordan Pond, as if it were the hub of a wheel. After you explore the Loop Road, bike the carriage roads, or climb one of the surrounding mountains, the cool shore of the pond provides welcome relief. A further incentive is the Jordan Pond House.

In 1896, Thomas A. McIntire and his wife bought a weather-beaten farmhouse on the southern shore of Jordan Pond. They began offering afternoon tea with hot popovers and fresh strawberry preserves, served on the lawn overlooking the water. Soon the Jordan Pond House became the place to gather each afternoon to relax and chat with friends over lunch or tea. John D. Rockefeller Jr. purchased the building in 1923 and donated it to the park in 1940. The McIntires continued to run the restaurant until 1945.

In 1979, the original building was destroyed by fire and was replaced by the present structure in 1982. Although the building is modern, the view, the popover recipe, and the tradition have not changed for more than a hundred years.

As you continue along the Loop Road beyond Jordan Pond, you will no doubt notice the large boulder that is precariously perched on the side of South Bubble. This is Bubble Rock.

The teahouse lawn offers a lovely view of the Bubbles.

The famous boulder perches precariously on the face of South Bubble.

Bubble Rock

Some twelve thousand years ago, as the glaciers melted away from this area, large boulders that had been frozen in the ice were gently lowered onto solid ground. These *glacial erratics*, as they are called, now litter the landscape of New England. Some of the most dramatic examples can be seen on the exposed summits of Acadia's mountains.

A short but steep trail climbs between the two Bubbles. From the summit of South Bubble there is a spectacular view overlooking Jordan Pond and stretching beyond, to the ocean. On the steep south face of the summit, you can get a closer look at Bubble Rock. An examination of this giant boulder reveals that its granite crystals do not match those of the mountain itself, which confirms that it was transported from some distant location by a glacier.

Will Bubble Rock ever fall? Look closely at the lip that keeps this rock balanced on the side of the mountain. Is it beginning to show signs of erosion? Will the weight of the rock someday overcome the force that holds it in place? What will happen when it does fall? Its destiny is for future generations to know.

After leaving the Bubble Rock trailhead, the Loop Road travels downhill several miles. At the bottom of the grade, a right-hand turn leads to Bubble Pond. (This is also another access point for the carriage road system.) As you enter the parking area at Bubble Pond, notice the beautiful stone bridge on your right.

Bubble Pond

Emerging from the random granite bedrock as if part of the natural landscape, Bubble Pond Bridge is one of sixteen such stone structures built as part of John D. Rockefeller Jr.'s carriage-road system. This bridge—like its counterparts elsewhere—reflects not only the care and artistry of the stonemasons who built it but also a philosophy of creating structures that fit into the landscape. These beautifully hand-crafted, granite bridges cross roads, streams, and valleys almost unnoticed. Each bridge is a unique work of art that complements in form and line the rocks, trees, and contours of the land that surrounds it.

If you walk across the bridge and follow the carriage road, it will bring you to the far end of the pond and, beyond that, to Day Mountain. A smaller bridal path follows the edge of the pond and eventually connects to the carriage road.

Nestled between Cadillac and Pemetic Mountains, the pond itself is small and narrow. Like all landforms on Mount Desert, the U-shaped valley that contains the pond reflects the handiwork of glaciers.

For the next three miles the Loop Road begins a long, gradual climb. On your left is Eagle Lake, the second largest body of fresh water on the island and the one that provides the drinking supply for the town of Bar Harbor. The next right will take you to the summit of Cadillac Mountain.

The pond was scooped out as a glacier passed between two mountains.

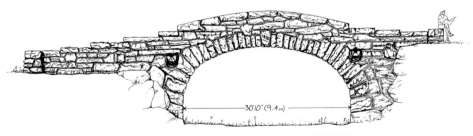

BUBBLE POND BRIDGE

The stone bridge complements its surroundings.

Cadillac Mountain

The 3.5-mile road toward the summit ascends the north and west faces of Cadillac (originally called Green) Mountain in a dramatic, meandering fashion. At each turn, a new vista beckons the driver to "take a look," but because traffic is two-way here, wait for a pull-off to enjoy the scenery. Plan to park in the lot at the top and spend an hour walking the half-mile trail that encircles the summit.

During April and May, or after a heavy rain, small waterfalls spring from the granite walls of the summit road. Their ephemeral nature is due to the mountain's shallow, rocky soil, which is unable to hold water. This characteristic is also one of the factors that limit the type and size of vegetation found on the mountain.

Cadillac's summit affords spectacular views in nearly all directions. To the north is inland Maine; to the east is the seemingly endless coastline; and to the south is the open Atlantic Ocean. The western view is best seen from the Blue Hill Overlook, which is a popular location for watching the sunset.

At 1,527 feet above sea level, the summit of Cadillac Mountain is the highest point on the Atlantic coast, but it is still well below the tree line. Why then is the top of the mountain not forested? The answer to this question is complex and not completely understood.

The fire of 1947 swept over this area and no doubt set back the growth of any vegetation. But even in 1604, when Champlain first viewed the island, the mountaintop was bare of trees. Logging, poor soil, hard granite bedrock, and cold, windy winters have all contributed to the lack of larger trees on Cadillac's summit (and the tops of most of the other mountains on the island).

The point that most people take to be the top of Mount Cadillac isn't actually the true summit, which lies behind the gift shop up an old path.

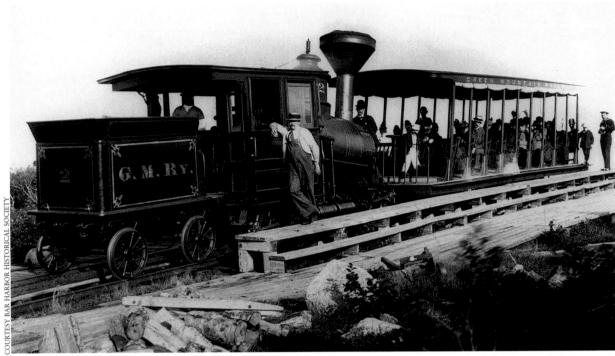

Rusticators rode the Green Mountain Railway to the summit.

Sparse vegetation adorns the mountaintop.

Few go to this spot because the views are not as rewarding. Nonetheless, it was the site of The Summit Hotel (1883–96), whose short life is no doubt attributable to the unpredictable weather and the inaccessibility of its location.

Getting to the top of Cadillac in the late 1800s involved either climbing a rough dirt road or taking the Cog Railway up the steep west slope of the mountain. Reaching the railway was an ordeal in itself, requiring a carriage ride to Eagle Lake, then a boat ride to the terminal at the far end of the lake. The modern summit road, built in the 1930s, makes Cadillac Mountain one of the most accessible and most visited mountaintops in America.

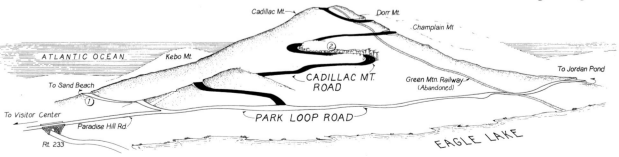

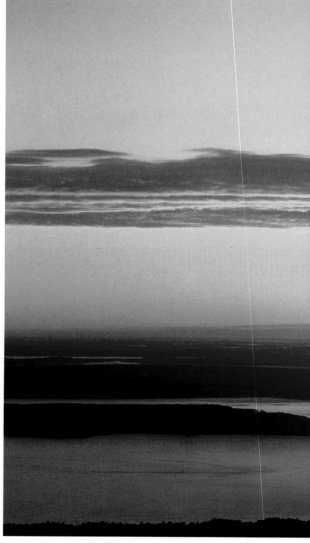

Cadillac's summit is the first place in the continental United States to see the sunrise from October 7 to March 6. (During the rest of the year, this honor is shared by Mars Hill and West Quoddy Head, both of which are also in down east Maine.) But whatever time you view the sunrise from this point, it is an experience worth the effort. Plan your visit carefully. Get to the summit early, as some of the most spectacular sights occur before the actual sunrise. Even in summer, the pre-dawn hours may be cool on the mountaintop. Wear warm clothing, bring your camera, and prepare for an event that you will not soon forget.

Upon descending the mountain, make a right turn on the Loop Road. After driving for a short distance, you will find yourself at the beginning of the circuit. Here, a left turn will take you back to the Visitor Center and from there to other points of interest beyond the Park Loop Road.

The view from Cadillac at dawn rewards the early riser.

Hiking Guide

Acadia has more than a hundred miles of hiking trails that vary in length and difficulty. Some are gentle wooded walks, others are challenging mountain climbs. Most mountain trails rise above the forest onto the open unprotected mountaintops. This list provides only the major routes that are accessible from the Loop Road. Before attempting any of these trails, you should seek more detailed information. A number of excellent guide books are available at the Acadia Visitor Center, at park headquarters, or at many local shops.

Before you begin hiking, you should know the type of trail you are on. Plan your time carefully. Bring something to drink. Choose appropriate footwear and clothing, and be prepared for changing conditions. Inform somebody where you are going and when you expect to return. Hike with a friend.

Trail	Trailhead	Distance (round trip in miles)	Rating
North Ridge of Cadillac	North Ridge Parking area	4.4	Moderate
Jessup Trail (to the Tarn)	Park Loop Road	1.8	Easy
Dorr Mountain	Sieur de Monts	3.0	Strenuous
Champlain North Ridge	Bear Brook Parking area	2.2	Moderate
Precipice	Precipice Parking area	1.6	Strenuous
Great Head	far side of Sand Beach	1.4	Moderate
Ocean Trail	upper parking lot at Sand Beach	3.6	Easy
Beehive	across the street from Sand Beach	1.0	Strenuous
Bowl and Beehive	across the street from Sand Beach	1.4	Moderate
Gorham Mountain	Gorham Mountain Parking area	2.0	Moderate
Jordan Pond Nature Trail	Jordan Pond Parking area	1.0	Easy
Jordan Pond Shore Path	Jordan Pond Parking area	3.3	Moderate
Penobscot Mountain	Jordan Pond Parking area	3.0	Strenuous
Sargent Mountain	Jordan Pond Parking area	5.0	Strenuous
Bubble Rock	Bubble Rock Parking area	1.2	Moderate
Pemetic Mountain	Bubble Pond Parking	2.4	Strenuous

Easy means that a person in moderately good physical condition would find this trail easy.
Moderate means that such a person would find this trail appropriate.
Strenuous means either that the trail is long or that somewhere on the trail there is steep climbing.

References

The following sources were used to confirm dates and facts for this book. All are recommended if you seek further information on the topics covered in these pages.

Chapman, Carleton A., *The Geology of Acadia National Park* (The Chatham Press, Inc., 1970)

Coffin, Tammis, editor, *The Rusticator's Journal* (Friends of Acadia, Bar Harbor, ME, 1993)

Collier, Sargent F., *Mount Desert Island & Acadia National Park: An Informal History* (Down East Books, Camden, ME, 1978)

Elfring, Chris, *AMC Guide to Mount Desert and Acadia National Park* (Appalachian Mountain Club Books, Boston, MA, 1993)

Gilman, Richard A., *The Geology of Mount Desert Island* (Maine Geological Survey Department of Conservation, 1986)

Gosner, Kenneth L., *A Field Guide to the Atlantic Seashore:* The Peterson Field Guide Series (Houghton Mifflin Co., Boston, MA, 1978)

Helfrich, G. W. and Gladys O'Neil, *Lost Bar Harbor* (Down East Books, Camden, ME, 1982)

Hill, Ruth Ann, *Discovering Old Bar Harbor and Acadia National Park* (Down East Books, Camden, ME, 1996)

Historic American Engineering Record, *Acadia National Park Roads & Bridges Report* (National Park Service, Bar Harbor, ME, 1995)

Jacobson, Bruce, *Acadia National Park Facts* (Acadia National Park, Bar Harbor, ME, 1996)

Kingsbury, John M., *The Rocky Shore* (The Chatham Press, Inc., Old Greenwich, CT, 1970)

Rieley, William D. and Roxanne S. Brouse, *Historic Resource Study for the Carriage Road System, Acadia National Park* (Rieley & Associates, Charlottesville, VA, 1989)

Roberts, Ann Rockefeller, *Mr. Rockefeller's Roads* (Down East Books, Camden, ME, 1990)

Rothe, Robert, *ACADIA: the Story Behind the Scenery* (KC Publications, Las Vegas, NV, 1979)

Woodside, David B., *The Story of Jordan Pond* (The Acadia Corporation, Bar Harbor, ME, 1996)

More good reading from Down East Books

If you enjoyed *Acadia's Park Loop Road,* **you'll want to know about these other Down East titles:**

Lost Bar Harbor, by G. W. Helfrich and Gladys O'Neil. The summer "cottages" of Mount Desert Island set a standard for luxury in the late nineteenth and early twentieth centuries. Here are eighty-six of the splendid structures that once graced the town of Bar Harbor. Some were lost to greed, some to pragmatism, and many to the great fire of 1947. Their like will not be seen again. 0-89272-142-1

Discovering Old Bar Harbor and Acadia National Park: An Unconventional History and Guide, by Ruth Ann Hill. The township of Bar Harbor encompasses more than a third of Mount Desert Island, including the most visited parts of Acadia National Park. Searching for Bar Harbor's past is a bit of a treasure hunt, but many things become evident once one knows where to look. This unusual guidebook tells just where to find traces of Bar Harbor's fascinating history. 0-89272-355-6

Mount Desert Island and Acadia National Park: An Informal History, photographs and text by Sargent F. Collier. The best from three classics about Bar Harbor, Mount Desert Island, and Acadia National Park. Edited by G. W. Helfrich. Heavily illustrated with the author, Sargent Collier's photographs of the contemporary scene and earlier prints of the good old days. 0-89272-044-1

Mr. Rockefeller's Roads: The Untold Story of Acadia's Carriage Roads & Their Creator, Ann Rockefeller Roberts. Acadia's fifty-one miles of carriage roads are the result of decades of personal effort by philanthropist John D. Rockefeller Jr. Here, JDR Jr.'s granddaughter recounts the fascinating story of Acadia's "Rockefeller Roads" and of a man ahead of his time. 0-89272-296-7

Acadia National Park: Maine's Intimate Parkland, photographs and text by Alan Nyiri. From its impressive vistas to its tiniest treasures, Acadia is an island parkland of haunting beauty. This magnificent collection of color photographs captures that beauty. 0-89272-219-3

Murder on Mount Desert, by David Rawson. A fast-moving plot, vivid local color, and plenty of action characterize this mystery/adventure novel set in the fictional town of Eagle Harbor on the "quiet side" of Mount Desert Island. Heart-stopping moments on the cliffs of Cadillac Mountain keep the plot line humming. 0-89272-363-7

The Mount Desert Island Pocket Guide Series
A Pocket Guide to Biking on Mt. Desert Island, by Audrey Shelton Minutolo. 0-89272-367-X
A Pocket Guide to Paddling the Waters of Mt. Desert Island, by Earl Brechlin. 0-89272-357-2
A Pocket Guide to Hiking on Mt. Desert Island, by Earl Brechlin. 0-89272-356-4
A Pocket Guide to the Carriage Roads of Acadia National Park, 2nd Edition, by Diana F. Abrell. 0-89272-349-1

Check your local bookstore, or order from Down East Books at 800-685-7962
Visa and MasterCard Accepted